NATIONAL FOOTBALL LEAGUE

★★★★ **NFL** ★★★★

DYNAMIC DUOS

by Tim Polzer

SCHOLASTIC INC.

New York   Toronto   London   Auckland   Sydney
Mexico City   New Delhi   Hong Kong   Buenos Aires

ISBN-13: 978-0-545-06556-6
ISBN-10: 0-545-06556-9

Published by Scholastic Inc.
SCHOLASTIC and associated logos are trademarks and/or registered trademarks of Scholastic Inc.

12 11 10 9 8 7 6 5 4 3 2 1   8 9 10 11 12/0

Designed by Cheung Tai
Printed in the U.S.A.
First printing, August 2008

TABLE OF CONTENTS

Tom Brady & Randy Moss

What happens when one of the gre[at] quarterbacks in NFL history is jo[ined with] one of the league's most ta[lent]ed receivers? Fans get to see a re[co]rd-breaking season. And that's just what happened when New England Patriots quarterback Tom Brady and receiver Randy Moss joined forces in 2007.

In the final game of the regular season, the undefeated Patriots were on the verge of making NFL history. They entered the game against the New York Giants with a record of 15-0 and hoped to join the 1972 Miami Dolphins as the second team to complete the regular season undefeated.

Other records were also on the line. Tom was only one touchdown away from tying Peyton Manning's record of 49 touchdown passes in a season. Randy was one touchdown catch from matching Jerry Rice's record of 22 touchdown receptions in a season.

It didn't take the Patriots pair long to close in on the records. In the first quarter, Tom found Randy in the end zone for a four-yard touchdown, tying both records. But the Giants were not giving up. As the game went on, the Patriots struggled to keep their unbeaten streak intact.

With the game on the line in the fourth quarter, Tom stepped back in the pocket and waited while Randy ran a deep pass route. Tom threw a long bomb that Randy caught and ran in for a 65-yard record-breaking touchdown—for both of them.

The touchdown also clinched a perfect regular season for the Patriots. It was the kind of exciting play the Patriots ned about when they traded for Randy in the off

The relationship began when Tom and the Patriots searched for ways to get better. Even though they had won three Super Bowls in six years, the team was looking to improve. First of all, they needed better receivers.

When the Patriots heard that Randy was not happy playing in Oakland, they were interested. After all, Randy was one of the few receivers with more than 100 touchdowns and more than 10,000 yards in his career. And Randy was excited about playing with Tom . . . and the chance to win a championship.

The trade surprised some fans who wondered if Randy would get along with Tom and the Patriots' coaches, but head coach Bill Belichick had no doubts. Randy wanted a Super Bowl ring, and he was determined to work hard and be a good teammate. As Tom and Randy spent hours running pass routes and practicing their timing, Coach Belichick called Randy the smartest receiver he had ever coached.

When the 2007 season kicked off, Tom and Randy quickly became the most dangerous pass–catch combo in the NFL. In Week 1, Tom completed 22 of 28 attempts for 297 yards and three touchdowns, including a 51-yard touchdown to Randy, in a 38-14 win over the New York Jets. The lopsided victory was the first of many.

But Randy wasn't the only receiver to thrive that year. Since Randy's speed caused defenses to double-cover him downfield, it opened up the middle for other receivers such as Wes Welker and Donte Stallworth.

As a result, Tom broke several of his own team passing records, and Randy helped the Patriots set an NFL season scoring record with 589 points in 16 games. That's an average of more than 36 points per game! The Pats also set a new NFL season record with 75 touchdowns.

While the Patriots did not win a fourth Super Bowl they will continue to make opposing defenses nervous as they contend for another Super Bowl championship.

Drew Brees & Marques Colston

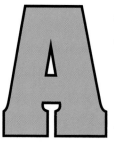

quarterback who needed a second chance and a receiver who needed a big break have helped the New Orleans Saints improve from last place to title contenders.

Quarterback Drew Brees grew up in a football family. His grandfather, Ray Akins, was one of the winningest high school football coaches in Texas history and his uncle, Marty Akins, was an All-America quarterback for the University of Texas Long-horns. Drew broke many passing records and won a state championship at Westlake High School in Austin, Texas, but most schools thought he was too small, so he accept-ed a scholarship to Purdue University. He went on to set more passing marks with the Boilermakers and joined the San Diego Chargers as the first pick of the second round of the NFL Draft in 2001.

Drew only played in one game as a rookie and struggled as a starter for several seasons. When the Chargers finished 4-12 in 2004, the team drafted another quarterback. Drew responded with one of the best performances among quar-terbacks that season, passing for more than 3,100 yards and 27 touchdowns. He was elected to the Pro Bowl and won the AFC Comeback Player of the Year award.

In the last game of the 2005 season, Drew injured his shoulder badly enough to have surgery. When he became a free agent, some teams were afraid that he could not recover from his injury. The Saints invited Drew to visit New Orleans, even though the city had been greatly damaged by a hurricane and flooding. After touring the destruction and listening to the Saints' rebuilding plan, Drew decided that he wanted to play for the team and help the city recover.

It turned out to be a great decision for Drew and the Saints. Drew thrived under the offensive scheme of new head coach Sean Payton. He led the Saints to the NFC Championship Game after completing 356 of 554 passes for an NFC record

4,418 yards, with 26 touchdowns and a passer rating of 96.2. He was voted a starter in the Pro Bowl and was selected first-team All-Pro.

Marques Colston had also made a habit of overcoming the odds. He was a good receiver in high school, but was very tall and thin, so most colleges were afraid to offer him a scholarship. He accepted an offer to play for Hofstra, a small school in New York, and went about trying to show other schools that they had made a mistake. Some NFL teams took notice of Marques catching 70 passes and nine touchdowns as a college senior, but he was still considered too slight to be drafted.

As the draft was about to end, Marques thought that he might go unselected until the Saints called his name as the fourth-to-last pick of the 2006 NFL Draft. While many seventh-round draft picks do not make the team's final roster, Marques worked hard and listened to the advice of Saints' coaches and veteran players. With those lessons, he played well enough to win a receiving job. In fact, Marques impressed the Saints so much that they traded away one of their best receivers to make a place for him.

Opposing teams were surprised how well Marques played in Coach Payton's passing offense. Drew learned to throw the ball high so Marques could outjump shorter defensive backs. He scored touchdowns in his first two games and produced great statistics. Marques finished with 70 catches and eight touchdowns, and led all rookies with 1,083 receiving yards.

Together, Drew and Marques give the Saints one of the most exciting passing duos in the NFL.

Ben Roethlisberger

& Hines Ward

Pittsburgh Steelers Ben Roethlisberger and Hines Ward make up one of the most consistently productive quarterback-receiver duos in the National Football League. They are also known as great team leaders.

At 6-feet-5 inches tall and 241 pounds, Ben is bigger than most quarterbacks, and he's earned the nickname of Big Ben. He was drafted out of the University of Miami of Ohio in 2004 and he quickly got a chance to prove himself. A few games into the 2004 season, an injury to starting quarterback Tommy Maddox made Ben the starting quarterback. He responded by playing like a veteran.

Ben became the first NFL rookie to win his first 13 regular-season games, and he broke several other records including Dan Marino's marks for rookie completion percentage (66.4) and passer ratings (98.1).

No Steelers quarterback, not even Pro Football Hall of Famer and NFL television announcer Terry Bradshaw, played better as a rookie. Ben not only won several Rookie of the Year awards, but helped lead the Steelers to Super Bowl XL against the Seattle Seahawks a year later.

While Ben made history as the youngest quarterback (23 years old) to win a Super Bowl, Super Bowl XL also gave Ben's favorite receiver a chance to shine. Hines says he was so nervous he couldn't sleep the night before his first Super Bowl, but you'd never have guessed it watching him play! He caught five receptions for 123 yards and was named the Most Valuable Player of Super Bowl XL.

What makes his achievement even more amazing is that Hines didn't always play receiver. When he arrived at the University of Georgia, it was as a quarterback. Later, he played running back before making one of the most successful transitions in NFL history. Some think that Hines' experience as a quarterback helps him think along with Ben as they read defensive coverages and change pass patterns. But he's also known for being one of the most ferocious blocking receivers ever, knocking defenders out of the way on running plays and clearing space for his teammates to score touchdowns.

He led the Steelers in receptions in just his second season, then surpassed the 1,000-yard mark and was voted to his first Pro Bowl in 2001. Once known as one of the NFL's underrated receivers, he has gone on to set almost every Steelers receiving record including 112 receptions in a season.

And he's proven that he's a big man off the field as well. After Super Bowl XL, Hines celebrated his victory by traveling to Seoul, South Koreas, his birthplace. There he created a foundation to fight discrimination.

Ben's third season didn't go as planned due to an accident in the offseason. But he was more determined than ever, and in the 2007 season, he threw 32 touchdown passes and helped lead the Steelers to the playoffs.

After the 2007 season, Ben signed a new long-term contract, so Ben and Hines will be playing catch for years to come.

Eli Manning & Plaxico Burress

When New York Giants quarterback Eli Manning needed to throw a touchdown to win Super Bowl XLII, he looked to receiver Plaxico Burress—and the rest is history.

With the Giants trailing the undefeated New England Patriots 14-10 and less than a minute remaining in the game, Eli found his favorite receiver in the corner of the end zone. His pass was true and Plaxico caught it for the touchdown that clinched the first NFL championship for both players.

Eli grew up watching his father, Archie, play quarterback for the New Orleans Saints. He attended the University of Mississippi, his father's alma mater, setting his own passing records there, then followed his older brother Peyton to the NFL.

Eli was selected number one by the San Diego Chargers in the first round of the 2004 NFL draft. But the Giants liked him so much that they traded draft picks to make him their quarterback of the future.

Like most young quarterbacks, Eli struggled to improve. His father and brother taught him to work hard on and off the field, but Giants fans were not always patient with his progress.

When head coach Tom Coughlin made Eli the starter midway through the 2004 season, the rookie was inconsistent, but he managed to help the Giants break an eight-game losing streak and gave fans reason to hope that he was on his way to becoming a good NFL quarterback.

Eli met their expectations in his second season by leading the Giants to the NFC East title. While Eli continued to show improvement, some critics believed that he was not as

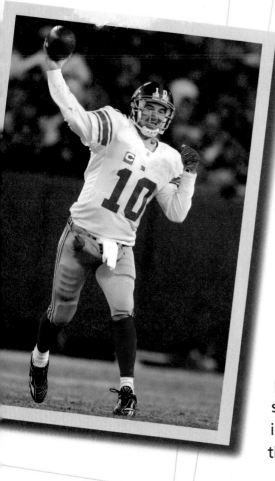

good as he should be. They pointed to his low completion percentage and quarterback efficiency rating, and the fact that his performance got worse late in the season.

Even though Eli led his team to another playoff berth, he felt the pressure of being a high draft pick and playing in the shadow of his big brother, Peyton. Giants fans wanted a great quarterback, not a passer who mostly threw short passes and too many interceptions. They also questioned his leadership ability.

When Eli began playing poorly in 2007, many Giants fans questioned his future with the team. But late in the season, the young quarterback helped turn the team around. He began taking more control of the team, reduced his mistakes, and gave up fewer interceptions.

He led the Giants to three playoff wins, including upsets of the favored Dallas Cowboys and Green Bay Packers. Eli and the Giants shocked everyone by making their way to Super Bowl XLII.

The Giants entered the big game as underdogs to the

highly favored Patriots. But Eli and the Giants remained confi-
dent. Plaxico was especially proud of his team's achievements
and told the media that the Giants would beat the Patriots.
Many fans shook their heads in disbelief, but Plaxico did not
back down.

The Giants had signed Plaxico from the Pittsburgh Steelers in 2005. He had been drafted out of Michigan State where
his height and leaping ability made him a big target for pass-
ers. Now, the Giants wanted a big-play receiver for Eli.

Plaxico also struggled at first in New York, where fans
and the media placed big expectations on his shoulders. When
the Giants lost, he often felt the
blame. But when the
Giants needed him in
the clutch, Plaxico al-
ways made the play.

In Super Bowl
XLII, the Patriots often
double-covered Plaxico,
so Eli threw most of his
passes to his other re-
ceivers.

But things looked
bleak for the Giants
when the Patriots scored
a touchdown to take a
14-10 lead with just over
two minutes remain-
ing. Getting the ball on
their own 17-yard line, the

Giants would need Eli to lead them 83 yards for a game-winning touch-down.

Eli responded by be-ing almost perfect. He showed poise in find-ing his receivers and kept calm under pres-sure. He especially revealed these traits on a play that won't soon be forgotten. On third down, the Patriots' pass rushers surrounded Eli and appeared to sack him, but the quar-terback shook off their tackles and escaped. He scrambled free and floated a pass downfield where receiver David Tyree leaped to make an unbelievable catch, holding the ball against his helmet as he fell to the field.

The amazing play kept the Giants game-winning drive alive and showed that Eli could make the big play under pressure.

A few plays later, Plaxico's Super Bowl prediction came true and Eli earned his place as a quarterback capable of leading his team to a Super Bowl victory.

Peyton Manning & Reggie Wayne

**P**eyton Manning owns many NFL passing records, but for a long time, fans wondered if he was good enough to lead the Indianapolis Colts to a championship. Reggie Wayne was one of the best receivers in the league, but it took a while for fans to notice. However, in 2007, Peyton and Reggie silenced the critics by winning Super Bowl XLI.

After entering the NFL as the number one draft pick in 1998, Peyton worked hard to make himself the Colts starting quarterback in his first season. He got his work ethic from his father, former NFL quarterback Archie Manning, and that attitude has helped him become one of the NFL's best quarterbacks.

After producing great passing statistics and earning Pro Bowl honors for several years, Peyton really made fans take notice in 2004. That's when Peyton threw 49 touchdown passes, breaking Dan Marino's longtime NFL record, and his passer rating of 121.1 set a new NFL record. Additionally, he set Colts' records for passing yardage—almost 5,000 yards. But when the Colts did not make the Super Bowl, Peyton remained unsatisfied. And fans questioned if he could win the "Big One."

During the next two seasons, Peyton continued to perfect his game, using more receivers and learning how to better audible, or change the play at the line of scrimmage. As the Colts improved their running game and defense, Peyton worked hard to limit his mistakes and interceptions. The hard work paid off when the Colts won the American Football Conference and earned their ticket to the Super Bowl to play the Chicago Bears.

In that game, Peyton showed that he could play in a big game, completing 25 of 38 attempts for 247 yards, including a 53-yard touchdown to Reggie in the first quarter. More important, Peyton did a good job of confusing the Bears' defense by changing the Colts' plays at the line. Peyton was voted the Most Valuable Player of Super Bowl XLI, and quieted his critics.

In 2007, Peyton and Reggie teamed up for another historic touchdown pass. Peyton's 59-yarder was his 288th career touchdown pass, breaking the Colts' record set by NFL legend Johnny Unitas. Afterward, he thanked his teammates and receivers, especially Reggie.

Reggie grew up in Louisiana where he played football and ran track in high school. He was twice named All-State and was offered a scholarship to play at the University of Miami, where he immediately became a starter for the Hurricanes. He played four seasons, set a school record with 173 career receptions, and scored more than 20 touchdowns.

Reggie was drafted by the Colts in 2001. Like most rookies, he struggled at first. He was fast, but he needed time to learn the ins and outs of being an NFL receiver. The Colts offense also used many receivers and tight ends, so he did not see many balls thrown his way. He caught just 27 passes and did not score a touchdown.

Reggie continued to work with Peyton and the Colts' coaches. That work paid off when Reggie almost doubled his receptions and scored four touchdowns in his second season.

Reggie really broke out during his third NFL season with 68 receptions for 838 yards and seven touchdowns. In his fourth season, Reggie truly became the receiving threat the Colts had wanted, catching 77 passes for more than 1,000 yards and scoring 12 touchdowns.

The Colts were so sure of Reggie's future that they offered him a new contract, and he responded with his best season ever, posting career highs with 86 receptions and 1,310 yards. To top it all off, Reggie was elected to his first Pro Bowl.

Today, Reggie is Peyton's first choice when the Colts need a long touchdown pass.

Tony Romo & Jason Witten

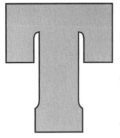wo of the NFL's newest stars are also best friends. Dallas Cowboys quarterback Tony Romo and tight end Jason Witten room together when the team is on the road and have become close friends away from the field. Their friendship has helped them become one of the NFL's best pass-and-catch combinations.

In 2003, Tony and Jason took very different paths to the NFL. Jason was a well-known tight end drafted in the third round out of the University of Tennessee. Tony was a lesser-known quarterback at a smaller school, Eastern Illinois University. Despite winning the Walter Payton Award, given to the nation's top player at the NCAA Division I-AA level, Tony went undrafted. Jason joined the Cowboys with expectations of becoming an immediate starter. Tony signed a free-agent contract with the Cowboys as a long-shot quarterback prospect.

In his first season, Jason had 35 receptions, the most of any NFL rookie tight end. In his first season, Tony ran the scout team as the Cowboys' third-string quarterback. The pair also became good friends off the field.

Jason showed off his quickness and pass-catching ability in his second season, leading NFC tight ends in receptions (87) and earning a spot in the Pro Bowl. Not only was Jason an excellent receiver, he also was a very good blocker on running plays. Tony continued to work hard learning the Cowboys' offense. He showed signs of improvement and moved his way up the Cowboys' roster to become backup quarterback to Drew Bledsoe.

Two seasons later, with Jason one of the league's best tight ends, it was time for Tony to join him as a Pro Bowl quarterback. ___ ames into the 2006 season, coach Bill Parcells named Tony the Cowboys' starting quarterback.

Tony quickly proved that he was up to the job. In fact, he ___rprised the NFL by leading the Cowboys to six wins and a wild-card playoff berth against the Seattle Seahawks. Trailing by 21–20 in the fourth quarter, Tony led the Cowboys down the field for a potential game-winning 19-yard field goal. As Tony, who also was the Cowboys' holder for field goals and extra points, lined up to receive the snap from center, his team seemed on the verge of winning the game—but Tony dropped the snap. The Cowboys lost the game and Tony was embarrassed, but he vowed to put the error behind him.

Tony bounced back with one of the greatest passing seasons in Cowboys history. He opened the 2007 season with four touchdown passes and a rushing touchdown against the New York Giants. Midway through his first full season as

the Cowboys' starting quarterback, Tony threw another four touchdown passes against the Packers in a victory over his childhood idol, Brett Favre.

Jason was a big part of the Cowboys passing offense, catching a career-high 96 passes for 1,145 yards and seven touchdowns. After leading all NFC tight ends in receptions, he was voted to his fourth Pro Bowl and was named to the All-Pro team for the first time in his career.

Tony finished the season by breaking Cowboys passing records for touchdowns and yards. In the final game of the regular season, Tony's pass to his buddy Jason set a new team season record with 335 completions. It was fitting that the two best friends had teamed up for another Cowboys record.

Tony's performance gave the Cowboys reason to sign him to a long-term contract that would make him the team's quarterback for many years. And because the Cowboys had signed a similar contract extension with Jason the previous year, the duo should be connecting on the field for many seasons to come.